Birding Journal

April 2018
from KP

©2015 by Wandering Walks of Wonder Publishing

Printed in the United States of America

All rights reserved. No part of this work covered by the copyrights hereon may be reproduced or used in any form or by any means – graphic, electronic or mechanical – without the prior written permission of the publishers, except for reviewers who may quote brief passages. Any request for photocopying, recording, taping or storage on information retrieval systems of any part of this work shall be directed in writing to the publisher.

The Publisher: Wandering Walks of Wonder Publishing

Kansas City, MO 64118

USA

Website: www.wanderingwalksofwonder.com

ISBN-13: 978-1519356239

ISBN-10: 1519356234

Bird Watching is a great way to escape the rat race and be one with nature. But, your bird watching experiences can fade with time. The best way to prevent this is to keep a bird watching diary for your sightings and trips.

Whether you are keeping track of the wild birds that visit your bird feeders or the birds in your nearest National Forest, your hobby will be enhanced by keeping a bird watching journal.

Experience show that recording what you see in your journal increases your focus on what you are watching. Watching becomes more than just seeing. It becomes an act of interpretation of what you are watching. Your journal can become a checklist to remind you what to look for.

Keeping a bird watching journal is a personal activity. It is entirely up to you what to include in your journal and no one should tell you how to keep one. There aren't any rules that you have to follow. You could simply keep a list of the bird species that you see, which is sometimes called a life list. To get the most out of your bird watching journal, you should write in it during and immediately after birding. Every sighting brings new experiences, even if you're just sitting in your backyard.

Date:	Species:	Time:
Day of Week:	Name:	☐ AM ☐ PM
Weather: ☐ Sunny ☐ Overcast ☐ Cloudy ☐ Rain ☐ Snow Air Temp:	Markings/Features: Behavior: Habitat:	Winds: ☐ Calm ☐ Mod. ☐ Heavy Barometer:

FIELD NOTES:
_____
_____
_____
_____
_____
_____
_____
_____

Date:	Species:	Time:
Day of Week:	Name:	☐ AM ☐ PM
Weather: ☐ Sunny ☐ Overcast ☐ Cloudy ☐ Rain ☐ Snow Air Temp:	Markings/Features: Behavior: Habitat:	Winds: ☐ Calm ☐ Mod. ☐ Heavy Barometer:

FIELD NOTES:

_____
_____
_____
_____
_____
_____
_____
_____
_____
_____

Date:	Species:	Time:
Day of Week:	Name:	☐ AM ☐ PM
Weather: ☐ Sunny ☐ Overcast ☐ Cloudy ☐ Rain ☐ Snow Air Temp:	Markings/Features: Behavior: Habitat:	Winds: ☐ Calm ☐ Mod. ☐ Heavy Barometer:

FIELD NOTES:

_____
_____
_____
_____
_____
_____
_____
_____
_____

Date:	Species:	Time:
Day of Week:	Name:	☐ AM ☐ PM
Weather: ☐ Sunny ☐ Overcast ☐ Cloudy ☐ Rain ☐ Snow Air Temp:	Markings/Features: Behavior: Habitat:	Winds: ☐ Calm ☐ Mod. ☐ Heavy Barometer:

FIELD NOTES:

_____
_____
_____
_____
_____
_____
_____
_____
_____

Date:	Species:	Time:
Day of Week:	Name:	☐ AM ☐ PM
Weather: ☐ Sunny ☐ Overcast ☐ Cloudy ☐ Rain ☐ Snow Air Temp:	Markings/Features: Behavior: Habitat:	Winds: ☐ Calm ☐ Mod. ☐ Heavy Barometer:

FIELD NOTES:

_____
_____
_____
_____
_____
_____
_____
_____

Date:	Species:	Time:
Day of Week:	Name:	☐ AM ☐ PM
Weather: ☐ Sunny ☐ Overcast ☐ Cloudy ☐ Rain ☐ Snow Air Temp:	Markings/Features: Behavior: Habitat:	Winds: ☐ Calm ☐ Mod. ☐ Heavy Barometer:

FIELD NOTES:

_____
_____
_____
_____
_____
_____
_____
_____
_____
_____
_____

Date:	Species:	Time:
Day of Week:	Name:	☐ AM ☐ PM
Weather: ☐ Sunny ☐ Overcast ☐ Cloudy ☐ Rain ☐ Snow Air Temp:	Markings/Features: Behavior: Habitat:	Winds: ☐ Calm ☐ Mod. ☐ Heavy Barometer:

FIELD NOTES:

_____
_____
_____
_____
_____
_____
_____
_____

Date:	Species:	Time:	
Day of Week:	Name:	☐	AM
		☐	PM

Weather:	Markings/Features:	Winds:	
☐ Sunny		☐	Calm
☐ Overcast		☐	Mod.
☐ Cloudy	Behavior:	☐	Heavy
☐ Rain			
☐ Snow			
	Habitat:		
Air Temp:		Barometer:	

FIELD NOTES:

_____
_____
_____
_____
_____
_____
_____
_____
_____

Date:	Species:	Time:
Day of Week:	Name:	☐ AM ☐ PM
Weather: ☐ Sunny ☐ Overcast ☐ Cloudy ☐ Rain ☐ Snow Air Temp:	Markings/Features: Behavior: Habitat:	Winds: ☐ Calm ☐ Mod. ☐ Heavy Barometer:

FIELD NOTES:

_____
_____
_____
_____
_____
_____
_____
_____

Date:	Species:	Time:
Day of Week:	Name:	☐ AM ☐ PM
Weather: ☐ Sunny ☐ Overcast ☐ Cloudy ☐ Rain ☐ Snow Air Temp:	Markings/Features: Behavior: Habitat:	Winds: ☐ Calm ☐ Mod. ☐ Heavy Barometer:

FIELD NOTES:

_____
_____
_____
_____
_____
_____
_____
_____
_____
_____

Date:	Species:	Time:
Day of Week:	Name:	☐ AM ☐ PM
Weather: ☐ Sunny ☐ Overcast ☐ Cloudy ☐ Rain ☐ Snow Air Temp:	Markings/Features: Behavior: Habitat:	Winds: ☐ Calm ☐ Mod. ☐ Heavy Barometer:

FIELD NOTES:

_____
_____
_____
_____
_____
_____
_____
_____

Date:	Species:	Time:
Day of Week:	Name:	☐ AM ☐ PM
Weather: ☐ Sunny ☐ Overcast ☐ Cloudy ☐ Rain ☐ Snow Air Temp:	Markings/Features: Behavior: Habitat:	Winds: ☐ Calm ☐ Mod. ☐ Heavy Barometer:

FIELD NOTES:

_____
_____
_____
_____
_____
_____
_____
_____
_____

Date:	Species:	Time:
Day of Week:	Name:	☐ AM ☐ PM
Weather: ☐ Sunny ☐ Overcast ☐ Cloudy ☐ Rain ☐ Snow Air Temp:	Markings/Features: Behavior: Habitat:	Winds: ☐ Calm ☐ Mod. ☐ Heavy Barometer:

FIELD NOTES:

_____
_____
_____
_____
_____
_____
_____
_____

Date:	Species:	Time:
Day of Week:	Name:	☐ AM ☐ PM
Weather: ☐ Sunny ☐ Overcast ☐ Cloudy ☐ Rain ☐ Snow Air Temp:	Markings/Features: Behavior: Habitat:	Winds: ☐ Calm ☐ Mod. ☐ Heavy Barometer:

FIELD NOTES:

_____
_____
_____
_____
_____
_____
_____
_____

Date:	Species:	Time:
Day of Week:	Name:	☐ AM ☐ PM
Weather: ☐ Sunny ☐ Overcast ☐ Cloudy ☐ Rain ☐ Snow Air Temp:	Markings/Features: Behavior: Habitat:	Winds: ☐ Calm ☐ Mod. ☐ Heavy Barometer:

FIELD NOTES:

_____
_____
_____
_____
_____
_____
_____
_____
_____

Date:	Species:	Time:
Day of Week:	Name:	☐ AM ☐ PM
Weather: ☐ Sunny ☐ Overcast ☐ Cloudy ☐ Rain ☐ Snow Air Temp:	Markings/Features: Behavior: Habitat:	Winds: ☐ Calm ☐ Mod. ☐ Heavy Barometer:

FIELD NOTES:

_____
_____
_____
_____
_____
_____
_____
_____
_____

Date:	Species:	Time:
Day of Week:	Name:	☐ AM ☐ PM
Weather: ☐ Sunny ☐ Overcast ☐ Cloudy ☐ Rain ☐ Snow Air Temp:	Markings/Features: Behavior: Habitat:	Winds: ☐ Calm ☐ Mod. ☐ Heavy Barometer:

FIELD NOTES:

_____
_____
_____
_____
_____
_____
_____
_____
_____

Date:	Species:	Time:
Day of Week:	Name:	☐ AM ☐ PM
Weather: ☐ Sunny ☐ Overcast ☐ Cloudy ☐ Rain ☐ Snow Air Temp:	Markings/Features: Behavior: Habitat:	Winds: ☐ Calm ☐ Mod. ☐ Heavy Barometer:

FIELD NOTES:

_____
_____
_____
_____
_____
_____
_____
_____

Date:	Species:	Time:
Day of Week:	Name:	☐ AM ☐ PM
Weather: ☐ Sunny ☐ Overcast ☐ Cloudy ☐ Rain ☐ Snow Air Temp:	Markings/Features: Behavior: Habitat:	Winds: ☐ Calm ☐ Mod. ☐ Heavy Barometer:

FIELD NOTES:

_____
_____
_____
_____
_____
_____
_____
_____
_____
_____

Date:	Species:	Time:	
Day of Week:	Name:	☐	AM
		☐	PM
Weather:	Markings/Features:	Winds:	
☐ Sunny		☐	Calm
☐ Overcast		☐	Mod.
☐ Cloudy	Behavior:	☐	Heavy
☐ Rain			
☐ Snow			
	Habitat:		
Air Temp:		Barometer:	

FIELD NOTES:

_____
_____
_____
_____
_____
_____
_____
_____
_____

Date:	Species:	Time:
Day of Week:	Name:	☐ AM ☐ PM
Weather: ☐ Sunny ☐ Overcast ☐ Cloudy ☐ Rain ☐ Snow Air Temp:	Markings/Features: Behavior: Habitat:	Winds: ☐ Calm ☐ Mod. ☐ Heavy Barometer:

FIELD NOTES:

_____
_____
_____
_____
_____
_____
_____
_____

Date:	Species:	Time:
Day of Week:	Name:	☐ AM ☐ PM
Weather: ☐ Sunny ☐ Overcast ☐ Cloudy ☐ Rain ☐ Snow Air Temp:	Markings/Features: Behavior: Habitat:	Winds: ☐ Calm ☐ Mod. ☐ Heavy Barometer:

FIELD NOTES:

_____

_____

_____

_____

_____

_____

_____

_____

_____

Date:	Species:	Time:
Day of Week:	Name:	☐ AM ☐ PM
Weather: ☐ Sunny ☐ Overcast ☐ Cloudy ☐ Rain ☐ Snow Air Temp:	Markings/Features: Behavior: Habitat:	Winds: ☐ Calm ☐ Mod. ☐ Heavy Barometer:

FIELD NOTES:

_____
_____
_____
_____
_____
_____
_____
_____
_____

Date:	Species:	Time:
Day of Week:	Name:	☐ AM ☐ PM
Weather: ☐ Sunny ☐ Overcast ☐ Cloudy ☐ Rain ☐ Snow Air Temp:	Markings/Features: Behavior: Habitat:	Winds: ☐ Calm ☐ Mod. ☐ Heavy Barometer:

FIELD NOTES:

_____
_____
_____
_____
_____
_____
_____
_____
_____

Date:	Species:	Time:
Day of Week:	Name:	☐ AM ☐ PM
Weather: ☐ Sunny ☐ Overcast ☐ Cloudy ☐ Rain ☐ Snow Air Temp:	Markings/Features: Behavior: Habitat:	Winds: ☐ Calm ☐ Mod. ☐ Heavy Barometer:

FIELD NOTES:

_____
_____
_____
_____
_____
_____
_____
_____

Date:	Species:	Time:
Day of Week:	Name:	☐ AM ☐ PM
Weather: ☐ Sunny ☐ Overcast ☐ Cloudy ☐ Rain ☐ Snow Air Temp:	Markings/Features: Behavior: Habitat:	Winds: ☐ Calm ☐ Mod. ☐ Heavy Barometer:

FIELD NOTES:

_____
_____
_____
_____
_____
_____
_____
_____
_____
_____

Date:	Species:	Time:
Day of Week:	Name:	☐ AM ☐ PM
Weather: ☐ Sunny ☐ Overcast ☐ Cloudy ☐ Rain ☐ Snow Air Temp:	Markings/Features: Behavior: Habitat:	Winds: ☐ Calm ☐ Mod. ☐ Heavy Barometer:

FIELD NOTES:

_____
_____
_____
_____
_____
_____
_____
_____
_____
_____

Date:	Species:	Time:
Day of Week:	Name:	☐ AM ☐ PM
Weather: ☐ Sunny ☐ Overcast ☐ Cloudy ☐ Rain ☐ Snow Air Temp:	Markings/Features: Behavior: Habitat:	Winds: ☐ Calm ☐ Mod. ☐ Heavy Barometer:

FIELD NOTES:

_____
_____
_____
_____
_____
_____
_____
_____
_____

Date:	Species:	Time:
Day of Week:	Name:	☐ AM ☐ PM
Weather: ☐ Sunny ☐ Overcast ☐ Cloudy ☐ Rain ☐ Snow Air Temp:	Markings/Features: Behavior: Habitat:	Winds: ☐ Calm ☐ Mod. ☐ Heavy Barometer:

FIELD NOTES:

_____
_____
_____
_____
_____
_____
_____
_____
_____

Date:	Species:	Time:
Day of Week:	Name:	☐ AM ☐ PM
Weather: ☐ Sunny ☐ Overcast ☐ Cloudy ☐ Rain ☐ Snow Air Temp:	Markings/Features: Behavior: Habitat:	Winds: ☐ Calm ☐ Mod. ☐ Heavy Barometer:

FIELD NOTES:
___
___
___
___
___
___
___
___
___

Date:	Species:	Time:
Day of Week:	Name:	☐ AM ☐ PM
Weather: ☐ Sunny ☐ Overcast ☐ Cloudy ☐ Rain ☐ Snow Air Temp:	Markings/Features: Behavior: Habitat:	Winds: ☐ Calm ☐ Mod. ☐ Heavy Barometer:

FIELD NOTES:

_____
_____
_____
_____
_____
_____
_____
_____
_____

Date:	Species:	Time:
Day of Week:	Name:	☐ AM ☐ PM
Weather: ☐ Sunny ☐ Overcast ☐ Cloudy ☐ Rain ☐ Snow Air Temp:	Markings/Features: Behavior: Habitat:	Winds: ☐ Calm ☐ Mod. ☐ Heavy Barometer:

FIELD NOTES:

_____
_____
_____
_____
_____
_____
_____
_____
_____

Date:	Species:	Time:
Day of Week:	Name:	☐ AM ☐ PM
Weather: ☐ Sunny ☐ Overcast ☐ Cloudy ☐ Rain ☐ Snow Air Temp:	Markings/Features: Behavior: Habitat:	Winds: ☐ Calm ☐ Mod. ☐ Heavy Barometer:

FIELD NOTES:

_____
_____
_____
_____
_____
_____
_____
_____
_____

Date:	Species:	Time:
Day of Week:	Name:	☐ AM ☐ PM
Weather: ☐ Sunny ☐ Overcast ☐ Cloudy ☐ Rain ☐ Snow Air Temp:	Markings/Features: Behavior: Habitat:	Winds: ☐ Calm ☐ Mod. ☐ Heavy Barometer:

FIELD NOTES:

_____
_____
_____
_____
_____
_____
_____
_____
_____

Date:	Species:	Time:
Day of Week:	Name:	☐ AM ☐ PM
Weather: ☐ Sunny ☐ Overcast ☐ Cloudy ☐ Rain ☐ Snow Air Temp:	Markings/Features: Behavior: Habitat:	Winds: ☐ Calm ☐ Mod. ☐ Heavy Barometer:

FIELD NOTES:

_____
_____
_____
_____
_____
_____
_____
_____
_____

Date:	Species:	Time:
Day of Week:	Name:	☐ AM ☐ PM
Weather: ☐ Sunny ☐ Overcast ☐ Cloudy ☐ Rain ☐ Snow Air Temp:	Markings/Features: Behavior: Habitat:	Winds: ☐ Calm ☐ Mod. ☐ Heavy Barometer:

FIELD NOTES:

_____
_____
_____
_____
_____
_____
_____
_____
_____

Date:	Species:	Time:
Day of Week:	Name:	☐ AM ☐ PM
Weather: ☐ Sunny ☐ Overcast ☐ Cloudy ☐ Rain ☐ Snow Air Temp:	Markings/Features: Behavior: Habitat:	Winds: ☐ Calm ☐ Mod. ☐ Heavy Barometer:

FIELD NOTES:

_____
_____
_____
_____
_____
_____
_____
_____

Date:	Species:	Time:
Day of Week:	Name:	☐ AM ☐ PM
Weather: ☐ Sunny ☐ Overcast ☐ Cloudy ☐ Rain ☐ Snow Air Temp:	Markings/Features: Behavior: Habitat:	Winds: ☐ Calm ☐ Mod. ☐ Heavy Barometer:

FIELD NOTES:

_____
_____
_____
_____
_____
_____
_____
_____

Date:	Species:	Time:
Day of Week:	Name:	☐ AM ☐ PM
Weather: ☐ Sunny ☐ Overcast ☐ Cloudy ☐ Rain ☐ Snow Air Temp:	Markings/Features: Behavior: Habitat:	Winds: ☐ Calm ☐ Mod. ☐ Heavy Barometer:

FIELD NOTES:

_____
_____
_____
_____
_____
_____
_____

Date:	Species:	Time:
Day of Week:	Name:	☐ AM ☐ PM
Weather: ☐ Sunny ☐ Overcast ☐ Cloudy ☐ Rain ☐ Snow Air Temp:	Markings/Features: Behavior: Habitat:	Winds: ☐ Calm ☐ Mod. ☐ Heavy Barometer:

FIELD NOTES:

_____
_____
_____
_____
_____
_____
_____
_____
_____

Date:	Species:	Time:
Day of Week:	Name:	☐ AM ☐ PM
Weather: ☐ Sunny ☐ Overcast ☐ Cloudy ☐ Rain ☐ Snow Air Temp:	Markings/Features: Behavior: Habitat:	Winds: ☐ Calm ☐ Mod. ☐ Heavy Barometer:

FIELD NOTES:

_____
_____
_____
_____
_____
_____
_____
_____

Date:	Species:	Time:
Day of Week:	Name:	☐ AM ☐ PM
Weather: ☐ Sunny ☐ Overcast ☐ Cloudy ☐ Rain ☐ Snow Air Temp:	Markings/Features: Behavior: Habitat:	Winds: ☐ Calm ☐ Mod. ☐ Heavy Barometer:

FIELD NOTES:

_____
_____
_____
_____
_____
_____
_____
_____
_____

Date:	Species:	Time:
Day of Week:	Name:	☐ AM ☐ PM
Weather: ☐ Sunny ☐ Overcast ☐ Cloudy ☐ Rain ☐ Snow Air Temp:	Markings/Features: Behavior: Habitat:	Winds: ☐ Calm ☐ Mod. ☐ Heavy Barometer:

FIELD NOTES:

_____
_____
_____
_____
_____
_____
_____
_____
_____

Date:	Species:	Time:
Day of Week:	Name:	☐ AM ☐ PM
Weather: ☐ Sunny ☐ Overcast ☐ Cloudy ☐ Rain ☐ Snow Air Temp:	Markings/Features: Behavior: Habitat:	Winds: ☐ Calm ☐ Mod. ☐ Heavy Barometer:

FIELD NOTES:

_____
_____
_____
_____
_____
_____
_____
_____
_____

Date:	Species:	Time:
Day of Week:	Name:	☐ AM ☐ PM
Weather: ☐ Sunny ☐ Overcast ☐ Cloudy ☐ Rain ☐ Snow Air Temp:	Markings/Features: Behavior: Habitat:	Winds: ☐ Calm ☐ Mod. ☐ Heavy Barometer:

FIELD NOTES:

_____
_____
_____
_____
_____
_____
_____
_____
_____

Date:	Species:	Time:
Day of Week:	Name:	☐ AM ☐ PM
Weather: ☐ Sunny ☐ Overcast ☐ Cloudy ☐ Rain ☐ Snow Air Temp:	Markings/Features: Behavior: Habitat:	Winds: ☐ Calm ☐ Mod. ☐ Heavy Barometer:

FIELD NOTES:

_____
_____
_____
_____
_____
_____
_____
_____
_____

Date:	Species:	Time:
Day of Week:	Name:	☐ AM ☐ PM
Weather: ☐ Sunny ☐ Overcast ☐ Cloudy ☐ Rain ☐ Snow Air Temp:	Markings/Features: Behavior: Habitat:	Winds: ☐ Calm ☐ Mod. ☐ Heavy Barometer:

FIELD NOTES:

_____
_____
_____
_____
_____
_____
_____
_____
_____

Date:	Species:	Time:
Day of Week:	Name:	☐ AM ☐ PM
Weather: ☐ Sunny ☐ Overcast ☐ Cloudy ☐ Rain ☐ Snow Air Temp:	Markings/Features: Behavior: Habitat:	Winds: ☐ Calm ☐ Mod. ☐ Heavy Barometer:

FIELD NOTES:

_____
_____
_____
_____
_____
_____
_____
_____

Date:	Species:	Time:
Day of Week:	Name:	☐ AM ☐ PM
Weather: ☐ Sunny ☐ Overcast ☐ Cloudy ☐ Rain ☐ Snow Air Temp:	Markings/Features: Behavior: Habitat:	Winds: ☐ Calm ☐ Mod. ☐ Heavy Barometer:

FIELD NOTES:

_____
_____
_____
_____
_____
_____
_____
_____

Date:	Species:	Time:
Day of Week:	Name:	☐ AM ☐ PM
Weather: ☐ Sunny ☐ Overcast ☐ Cloudy ☐ Rain ☐ Snow Air Temp:	Markings/Features: Behavior: Habitat:	Winds: ☐ Calm ☐ Mod. ☐ Heavy Barometer:

FIELD NOTES:

_____
_____
_____
_____
_____
_____
_____
_____

Date:	Species:	Time:
Day of Week:	Name:	☐ AM ☐ PM
Weather: ☐ Sunny ☐ Overcast ☐ Cloudy ☐ Rain ☐ Snow Air Temp:	Markings/Features: Behavior: Habitat:	Winds: ☐ Calm ☐ Mod. ☐ Heavy Barometer:

FIELD NOTES:

_____
_____
_____
_____
_____
_____
_____
_____
_____

Date:	Species:	Time:
Day of Week:	Name:	☐ AM ☐ PM
Weather: ☐ Sunny ☐ Overcast ☐ Cloudy ☐ Rain ☐ Snow Air Temp:	Markings/Features: Behavior: Habitat:	Winds: ☐ Calm ☐ Mod. ☐ Heavy Barometer:

FIELD NOTES:

_____
_____
_____
_____
_____
_____
_____
_____
_____

Date:	Species:	Time:
Day of Week:	Name:	☐ AM ☐ PM
Weather: ☐ Sunny ☐ Overcast ☐ Cloudy ☐ Rain ☐ Snow Air Temp:	Markings/Features: Behavior: Habitat:	Winds: ☐ Calm ☐ Mod. ☐ Heavy Barometer:

FIELD NOTES:

_____
_____
_____
_____
_____
_____
_____
_____
_____

Date:	Species:	Time:
Day of Week:	Name:	☐ AM ☐ PM
Weather: ☐ Sunny ☐ Overcast ☐ Cloudy ☐ Rain ☐ Snow Air Temp:	Markings/Features: Behavior: Habitat:	Winds: ☐ Calm ☐ Mod. ☐ Heavy Barometer:

FIELD NOTES:

_____
_____
_____
_____
_____
_____
_____
_____
_____

Date:	Species:	Time:
Day of Week:	Name:	☐ AM ☐ PM
Weather: ☐ Sunny ☐ Overcast ☐ Cloudy ☐ Rain ☐ Snow Air Temp:	Markings/Features: Behavior: Habitat:	Winds: ☐ Calm ☐ Mod. ☐ Heavy Barometer:

FIELD NOTES:

_____
_____
_____
_____
_____
_____
_____
_____
_____

Date:	Species:	Time:
Day of Week:	Name:	☐ AM ☐ PM
Weather: ☐ Sunny ☐ Overcast ☐ Cloudy ☐ Rain ☐ Snow Air Temp:	Markings/Features: Behavior: Habitat:	Winds: ☐ Calm ☐ Mod. ☐ Heavy Barometer:

FIELD NOTES:

_____
_____
_____
_____
_____
_____
_____
_____
_____

Date:	Species:	Time:
Day of Week:	Name:	☐ AM ☐ PM
Weather: ☐ Sunny ☐ Overcast ☐ Cloudy ☐ Rain ☐ Snow Air Temp:	Markings/Features: Behavior: Habitat:	Winds: ☐ Calm ☐ Mod. ☐ Heavy Barometer:

FIELD NOTES:

_____
_____
_____
_____
_____
_____
_____
_____

Date:	Species:	Time:	
Day of Week:	Name:	☐	AM
		☐	PM

Weather:	Markings/Features:	Winds:	
☐ Sunny		☐	Calm
☐ Overcast		☐	Mod.
☐ Cloudy	Behavior:	☐	Heavy
☐ Rain			
☐ Snow			
	Habitat:		
Air Temp:		Barometer:	

FIELD NOTES:

_____
_____
_____
_____
_____
_____
_____
_____
_____

Date:	Species:	Time:
Day of Week:	Name:	☐ AM ☐ PM
Weather: ☐ Sunny ☐ Overcast ☐ Cloudy ☐ Rain ☐ Snow Air Temp:	Markings/Features: Behavior: Habitat:	Winds: ☐ Calm ☐ Mod. ☐ Heavy Barometer:

FIELD NOTES:

_____
_____
_____
_____
_____
_____
_____
_____
_____

Date:	Species:	Time:
Day of Week:	Name:	☐ AM ☐ PM
Weather: ☐ Sunny ☐ Overcast ☐ Cloudy ☐ Rain ☐ Snow Air Temp:	Markings/Features: Behavior: Habitat:	Winds: ☐ Calm ☐ Mod. ☐ Heavy Barometer:

FIELD NOTES:

_____
_____
_____
_____
_____
_____
_____
_____

Date:	Species:	Time:
Day of Week:	Name:	☐ AM ☐ PM
Weather: ☐ Sunny ☐ Overcast ☐ Cloudy ☐ Rain ☐ Snow Air Temp:	Markings/Features: Behavior: Habitat:	Winds: ☐ Calm ☐ Mod. ☐ Heavy Barometer:

FIELD NOTES:

_____
_____
_____
_____
_____
_____
_____
_____

Date:	Species:	Time:
Day of Week:	Name:	☐ AM ☐ PM
Weather: ☐ Sunny ☐ Overcast ☐ Cloudy ☐ Rain ☐ Snow Air Temp:	Markings/Features: Behavior: Habitat:	Winds: ☐ Calm ☐ Mod. ☐ Heavy Barometer:

FIELD NOTES:

_____
_____
_____
_____
_____
_____
_____
_____

Date:	Species:	Time:
Day of Week:	Name:	☐ AM ☐ PM
Weather: ☐ Sunny ☐ Overcast ☐ Cloudy ☐ Rain ☐ Snow Air Temp:	Markings/Features: Behavior: Habitat:	Winds: ☐ Calm ☐ Mod. ☐ Heavy Barometer:

FIELD NOTES:

_____
_____
_____
_____
_____
_____
_____
_____
_____

Date:	Species:	Time:
Day of Week:	Name:	☐ AM ☐ PM
Weather: ☐ Sunny ☐ Overcast ☐ Cloudy ☐ Rain ☐ Snow Air Temp:	Markings/Features: Behavior: Habitat:	Winds: ☐ Calm ☐ Mod. ☐ Heavy Barometer:

FIELD NOTES:

_____
_____
_____
_____
_____
_____
_____
_____
_____

Date:	Species:	Time:
Day of Week:	Name:	☐ AM ☐ PM
Weather: ☐ Sunny ☐ Overcast ☐ Cloudy ☐ Rain ☐ Snow Air Temp:	Markings/Features: Behavior: Habitat:	Winds: ☐ Calm ☐ Mod. ☐ Heavy Barometer:

FIELD NOTES:

_____
_____
_____
_____
_____
_____
_____
_____
_____
_____

Date:	Species:	Time:
Day of Week:	Name:	☐ AM ☐ PM
Weather: ☐ Sunny ☐ Overcast ☐ Cloudy ☐ Rain ☐ Snow Air Temp:	Markings/Features: Behavior: Habitat:	Winds: ☐ Calm ☐ Mod. ☐ Heavy Barometer:

FIELD NOTES:

_____
_____
_____
_____
_____
_____
_____
_____
_____
_____

Date:	Species:	Time:
Day of Week:	Name:	☐ AM ☐ PM
Weather: ☐ Sunny ☐ Overcast ☐ Cloudy ☐ Rain ☐ Snow Air Temp:	Markings/Features: Behavior: Habitat:	Winds: ☐ Calm ☐ Mod. ☐ Heavy Barometer:

FIELD NOTES:

_____
_____
_____
_____
_____
_____
_____
_____
_____

Date:	Species:	Time:
Day of Week:	Name:	☐ AM ☐ PM
Weather: ☐ Sunny ☐ Overcast ☐ Cloudy ☐ Rain ☐ Snow Air Temp:	Markings/Features: Behavior: Habitat:	Winds: ☐ Calm ☐ Mod. ☐ Heavy Barometer:

FIELD NOTES:

_____
_____
_____
_____
_____
_____
_____
_____
_____
_____

Date:	Species:	Time:
Day of Week:	Name:	☐ AM ☐ PM
Weather: ☐ Sunny ☐ Overcast ☐ Cloudy ☐ Rain ☐ Snow Air Temp:	Markings/Features: Behavior: Habitat:	Winds: ☐ Calm ☐ Mod. ☐ Heavy Barometer:

FIELD NOTES:

_____
_____
_____
_____
_____
_____
_____
_____
_____

Date:	Species:	Time:
Day of Week:	Name:	☐ AM ☐ PM
Weather: ☐ Sunny ☐ Overcast ☐ Cloudy ☐ Rain ☐ Snow Air Temp:	Markings/Features: Behavior: Habitat:	Winds: ☐ Calm ☐ Mod. ☐ Heavy Barometer:

FIELD NOTES:

_____
_____
_____
_____
_____
_____
_____
_____

Date:	Species:	Time:
Day of Week:	Name:	☐ AM ☐ PM
Weather: ☐ Sunny ☐ Overcast ☐ Cloudy ☐ Rain ☐ Snow Air Temp:	Markings/Features: Behavior: Habitat:	Winds: ☐ Calm ☐ Mod. ☐ Heavy Barometer:

FIELD NOTES:
_____
_____
_____
_____
_____
_____
_____
_____
_____

Birding Life List

Ducks, Geese, and Swans (Anatidae)	Black-bellied Whistling-Duck	
	Fulvous Whistling-Duck	
	Taiga Bean-Goose	
	Tundra Bean-Goose	
	Pink-footed Goose	
	Greater White-fronted Goose	
	Lesser White-fronted Goose	
	Graylag Goose	
	Emperor Goose	
	Snow Goose	
	Ross's Goose	
	Brant	
	Barnacle Goose	
	Cackling Goose	
	Canada Goose	
	Mute Swan	
	Trumpeter Swan	
	Tundra Swan	
	Whooper Swan	
	Egyptian Goose	
	Muscovy Duck	
	Wood Duck	
	Gadwall	
	Falcated Duck	
	Eurasian Wigeon	
	American Wigeon	
	American Black Duck	
	Mallard	
	Mottled Duck	
	Eastern Spot-billed Duck	
	Blue-winged Teal	
	Cinnamon Teal	

	Northern Shoveler	
	White-cheeked Pintail	
	Northern Pintail	
	Garganey	
	Baikal Teal	
	Green-winged Teal	
	Canvasback	
	Redhead	
	Common Pochard	
	Ring-necked Duck	
	Tufted Duck	
	Greater Scaup	
	Lesser Scaup	
	Steller's Eider	
	Spectacled Eider	
	King Eider	
	Common Eider	
	Harlequin Duck	
	Labrador Duck	
	Surf Scoter	
	White-winged Scoter	
	Black Scoter	
	Long-tailed Duck	
	Bufflehead	
	Common Goldeneye	
	Barrow's Goldeneye	
	Smew	
	Hooded Merganser	
	Common Merganser	
	Red-breasted Merganser	
	Masked Duck	
	Ruddy Duck	

Curassows and Guans (Cracidae)	Plain Chachalaca	
New World Quail (Odontophoridae)	Mountain Quail	
	Scaled Quail	
	California Quail	
	Gambel's Quail	
	Northern Bobwhite	
	Montezuma Quail	
Partridges, Grouse, Turkeys, and Old World Quail (Phasianidae)	Chukar	
	Himalayan Snowcock	
	Gray Partridge	
	Ring-necked Pheasant	
	Ruffed Grouse	
	Greater Sage-Grouse	
	Gunnison Sage-Grouse	
	Spruce Grouse	
	Willow Ptarmigan	
	Rock Ptarmigan	
	White-tailed Ptarmigan	
	Dusky Grouse	
	Sooty Grouse	
	Sharp-tailed Grouse	
	Greater Prairie-Chicken	
	Lesser Prairie-Chicken	
	Wild Turkey	
Loons (Gaviidae)	Red-throated Loon	
	Arctic Loon	
	Pacific Loon	
	Common Loon	
	Yellow-billed Loon	

Family	Species	
Grebes (Podicipedidae)	Least Grebe	
	Pied-billed Grebe	
	Horned Grebe	
	Red-necked Grebe	
	Eared Grebe	
	Western Grebe	
	Clark's Grebe	
Flamingos (Phoenicopteridae)	American Flamingo	
Albatrosses (Diomedeidae)	Yellow-nosed Albatross	
	White-capped Albatross	
	Salvin's Albatross	
	Black-browed Albatross	
	Light-mantled Albatross	
	Wandering Albatross	
	Laysan Albatross	
	Black-footed Albatross	
	Short-tailed Albatross	
Shearwaters and Petrels (Procellariidae)	Northern Fulmar	
	Great-winged Petrel	
	Providence Petrel	
	Trindade Petrel	
	Murphy's Petrel	
	Mottled Petrel	
	Bermuda Petrel	
	Black-capped Petrel	
	Hawaiian Petrel	
	Fea's Petrel	
	Zino's Petrel	
	Cook's Petrel	
	Stejneger's Petrel	
	Bulwer's Petrel	
	White-chinned Petrel	

	Parkinson's Petrel	
	Streaked Shearwater	
	Cory's Shearwater	
	Cape Verde Shearwater	
	Pink-footed Shearwater	
	Flesh-footed Shearwater	
	Great Shearwater	
	Wedge-tailed Shearwater	
	Buller's Shearwater	
	Sooty Shearwater	
	Short-tailed Shearwater	
	Manx Shearwater	
	Newell's Shearwater	
	Black-vented Shearwater	
	Audubon's Shearwater	
	Barolo Shearwater	
Storm-Petrels (Hydrobatidae)	Wilson's Storm-Petrel	
	White-faced Storm-Petrel	
	European Storm-Petrel	
	Black-bellied Storm-Petrel	
	Fork-tailed Storm-Petrel	
	Ringed Storm-Petrel	
	Swinhoe's Storm-Petrel	
	Leach's Storm-Petrel	
	Ashy Storm-Petrel	
	Band-rumped Storm-Petrel	
	Wedge-rumped Storm-Petrel	
	Black Storm-Petrel	
	Tristram's Storm-Petrel	
	Least Storm-Petrel	

Family	Species	
Tropicbirds (Phaethontidae)	White-tailed Tropicbird	
	Red-billed Tropicbird	
	Red-tailed Tropicbird	
Storks (Ciconiidae)	Jabiru	
	Wood Stork	
Frigatebirds (Fregatidae)	Magnificent Frigatebird	
	Great Frigatebird	
	Lesser Frigatebird	
Boobies and Gannets (Sulidae)	Masked Booby	
	Blue-footed Booby	
	Brown Booby	
	Red-footed Booby	
	Northern Gannet	
Cormorants (Phalacrocoracidae)	Brandt's Cormorant	
	Neotropic Cormorant	
	Double-crested Cormorant	
	Great Cormorant	
	Red-faced Cormorant	
	Pelagic Cormorant	
Darters (Anhingidae)	Anhinga	
Pelicans (Pelecanidae)	American White Pelican	
	Brown Pelican	
Bitterns, Herons, and Allies (Ardeidae)	American Bittern	
	Yellow Bittern	
	Least Bittern	
	Bare-throated Tiger-Heron	
	Great Blue Heron	
	Gray Heron	
	Great Egret	
	Intermediate Egret	
	Chinese Egret	
	Little Egret	

	Western Reef-Heron	
	Snowy Egret	
	Little Blue Heron	
	Tricolored Heron	
	Reddish Egret	
	Cattle Egret	
	Chinese Pond-Heron	
	Green Heron	
	Black-crowned Night-Heron	
	Yellow-crowned Night-Heron	
Ibises and Spoonbills (Threskiornithidae)	White Ibis	
	Scarlet Ibis	
	Glossy Ibis	
	White-faced Ibis	
	Roseate Spoonbill	
New World Vultures (Cathartidae)	Black Vulture	
	Turkey Vulture	
	California Condor	
Ospreys (Pandionidae)	Osprey	
Hawks, Kites, Eagles, and Allies (Accipitridae)	Hook-billed Kite	
	Swallow-tailed Kite	
	White-tailed Kite	
	Snail Kite	
	Double-toothed Kite	
	Mississippi Kite	
	Bald Eagle	
	White-tailed Eagle	
	Steller's Sea-Eagle	
	Northern Harrier	
	Sharp-shinned Hawk	
	Cooper's Hawk	
	Northern Goshawk	

	Crane Hawk	
	Common Black Hawk	
	Roadside Hawk	
	Harris's Hawk	
	White-tailed Hawk	
	Gray Hawk	
	Red-shouldered Hawk	
	Broad-winged Hawk	
	Short-tailed Hawk	
	Swainson's Hawk	
	Zone-tailed Hawk	
	Red-tailed Hawk	
	Rough-legged Hawk	
	Ferruginous Hawk	
	Golden Eagle	
Rails, Gallinules, and Coots (Rallidae)	Yellow Rail	
	Black Rail	
	Corn Crake	
	Ridgway's Rail	
	Clapper Rail	
	King Rail	
	Virginia Rail	
	Rufous-necked Wood-Rail	
	Sora	
	Paint-billed Crake	
	Spotted Rail	
	Purple Swamphen	
	Purple Gallinule	
	Common Gallinule	
	Common Moorhen	
	Eurasian Coot	
	American Coot	

Sungrebes (Heliornithidae)	Sungrebe	
Limpkins (Aramidae)	Limpkin	
Cranes (Gruidae)	Sandhill Crane	
	Common Crane	
	Whooping Crane	
Thick-knees (Burhinidae)	Double-striped Thick-knee	
Stilts and Avocets (Recurvirostridae)	Black-winged Stilt	
	Black-necked Stilt	
	American Avocet	
Oystercatchers (Haematopodidae)	Eurasian Oystercatcher	
	American Oystercatcher	
	Black Oystercatcher	
Lapwings and Plovers (Charadriidae)	Northern Lapwing	
	Black-bellied Plover	
	European Golden-Plover	
	American Golden-Plover	
	Pacific Golden-Plover	
	Lesser Sand-Plover	
	Greater Sand-Plover	
	Collared Plover	
	Snowy Plover	
	Wilson's Plover	
	Common Ringed Plover	
	Semipalmated Plover	
	Piping Plover	
	Little Ringed Plover	
	Killdeer	
	Mountain Plover	
	Eurasian Dotterel	
Jacanas (Jacanidae)	Northern Jacana	

Sandpipers, Phalaropes, and Allies (Scolopacidae)	Terek Sandpiper	
	Common Sandpiper	
	Spotted Sandpiper	
	Green Sandpiper	
	Solitary Sandpiper	
	Gray-tailed Tattler	
	Wandering Tattler	
	Spotted Redshank	
	Greater Yellowlegs	
	Common Greenshank	
	Willet	
	Lesser Yellowlegs	
	Marsh Sandpiper	
	Wood Sandpiper	
	Common Redshank	
	Upland Sandpiper	
	Little Curlew	
	Eskimo Curlew	
	Whimbrel	
	Bristle-thighed Curlew	
	Far Eastern Curlew	
	Slender-billed Curlew	
	Eurasian Curlew	
	Long-billed Curlew	
	Black-tailed Godwit	
	Hudsonian Godwit	
	Bar-tailed Godwit	
	Marbled Godwit	
	Ruddy Turnstone	
	Black Turnstone	
	Great Knot	
	Red Knot	

	Surfbird	
	Ruff	
	Broad-billed Sandpiper	
	Sharp-tailed Sandpiper	
	Stilt Sandpiper	
	Curlew Sandpiper	
	Temminck's Stint	
	Long-toed Stint	
	Spoon-billed Sandpiper	
	Red-necked Stint	
	Sanderling	
	Dunlin	
	Rock Sandpiper	
	Purple Sandpiper	
	Baird's Sandpiper	
	Little Stint	
	Least Sandpiper	
	White-rumped Sandpiper	
	Buff-breasted Sandpiper	
	Pectoral Sandpiper	
	Semipalmated Sandpiper	
	Western Sandpiper	
	Short-billed Dowitcher	
	Long-billed Dowitcher	
	Jack Snipe	
	Wilson's Snipe	
	Common Snipe	
	Pin-tailed Snipe	
	Solitary Snipe	
	Eurasian Woodcock	
	American Woodcock	
	Wilson's Phalarope	

Pratincoles (Glareolidae)	Oriental Pratincole	
Skuas and Jaegers (Stercorariidae)	Great Skua	
	South Polar Skua	
	Pomarine Jaeger	
	Parasitic Jaeger	
	Long-tailed Jaeger	
Auks, Murres, and Puffins (Alcidae)	Dovekie	
	Common Murre	
	Thick-billed Murre	
	Razorbill	
	Great Auk	
	Black Guillemot	
	Pigeon Guillemot	
	Long-billed Murrelet	
	Marbled Murrelet	
	Kittlitz's Murrelet	
	Scripps's Murrelet	
	Guadalupe Murrelet	
	Craveri's Murrelet	
	Ancient Murrelet	
	Cassin's Auklet	
	Parakeet Auklet	
	Least Auklet	
	Whiskered Auklet	
	Crested Auklet	
	Rhinoceros Auklet	
	Atlantic Puffin	
	Horned Puffin	
	Tufted Puffin	

Gulls, Terns, and Skimmers (Laridae)	Swallow-tailed Gull	
	Black-legged Kittiwake	
	Red-legged Kittiwake	
	Ivory Gull	
	Sabine's Gull	
	Bonaparte's Gull	
	Gray-hooded Gull	
	Black-headed Gull	
	Little Gull	
	Ross's Gull	
	Laughing Gull	
	Franklin's Gull	
	Belcher's Gull	
	Black-tailed Gull	
	Heermann's Gull	
	Mew Gull	
	Ring-billed Gull	
	Western Gull	
	Yellow-footed Gull	
	California Gull	
	Herring Gull	
	Yellow-legged Gull	
	Thayer's Gull	
	Iceland Gull	
	Lesser Black-backed Gull	
	Slaty-backed Gull	
	Glaucous-winged Gull	
	Glaucous Gull	
	Great Black-backed Gull	
	Kelp Gull	
	Brown Noddy	
	Black Noddy	

	Sooty Tern		
	Bridled Tern		
	Aleutian Tern		
	Least Tern		
	Large-billed Tern		
	Gull-billed Tern		
	Caspian Tern		
	Black Tern		
	White-winged Tern		
	Whiskered Tern		
	Roseate Tern		
	Common Tern		
	Arctic Tern		
	Forster's Tern		
	Royal Tern		
	Sandwich Tern		
	Elegant Tern		
	Black Skimmer		
Pigeons and Doves (Columbidae)	Rock Pigeon		
	Scaly-naped Pigeon		
	White-crowned Pigeon		
	Red-billed Pigeon		
	Band-tailed Pigeon		
	Oriental Turtle-Dove		
	European Turtle-Dove		
	Eurasian Collared-Dove		
	Spotted Dove		
	Passenger Pigeon		
	Inca Dove		
	Common Ground-Dove		
	Ruddy Ground-Dove		
	Ruddy Quail-Dove		

	Key West Quail-Dove	
	White-tipped Dove	
	White-winged Dove	
	Zenaida Dove	
	Mourning Dove	
Cuckoos, Roadrunners, and Anis (Cuculidae)	Common Cuckoo	
	Oriental Cuckoo	
	Yellow-billed Cuckoo	
	Mangrove Cuckoo	
	Black-billed Cuckoo	
	Greater Roadrunner	
	Smooth-billed Ani	
	Groove-billed Ani	
Barn Owls (Tytonidae)	Barn Owl	
Typical Owls (Strigidae)	Flammulated Owl	
	Oriental Scops-Owl	
	Western Screech-Owl	
	Eastern Screech-Owl	
	Whiskered Screech-Owl	
	Great Horned Owl	
	Snowy Owl	
	Northern Hawk Owl	
	Northern Pygmy-Owl	
	Ferruginous Pygmy-Owl	
	Elf Owl	
	Burrowing Owl	
	Mottled Owl	
	Spotted Owl	
	Barred Owl	
	Great Gray Owl	
	Long-eared Owl	
	Stygian Owl	

	Short-eared Owl		
	Boreal Owl		
	Northern Saw-whet Owl		
	Northern Boobook		
Goatsuckers (Caprimulgidae)	Lesser Nighthawk		
	Common Nighthawk		
	Antillean Nighthawk		
	Common Pauraque		
	Common Poorwill		
	Chuck-will's-widow		
	Buff-collared Nightjar		
	Eastern Whip-poor-will		
	Mexican Whip-poor-will		
	Gray Nightjar		
Swifts (Apodidae)	Black Swift		
	White-collared Swift		
	Chimney Swift		
	Vaux's Swift		
	White-throated Needletail		
	Common Swift		
	Fork-tailed Swift		
	White-throated Swift		
	Antillean Palm-Swift		
Hummingbirds (Trochilidae)	Green Violetear		
	Green-breasted Mango		
	Magnificent Hummingbird		
	Plain-capped Starthroat		
	Blue-throated Hummingbird		
	Bahama Woodstar		
	Lucifer Hummingbird		
	Ruby-throated Hummingbird		
	Black-chinned Hummingbird		

		Anna's Hummingbird	
		Costa's Hummingbird	
		Bumblebee Hummingbird	
		Broad-tailed Hummingbird	
		Rufous Hummingbird	
		Allen's Hummingbird	
		Calliope Hummingbird	
		Broad-billed Hummingbird	
		Berylline Hummingbird	
		Buff-bellied Hummingbird	
		Cinnamon Hummingbird	
		Violet-crowned Hummingbird	
		White-eared Hummingbird	
		Xantus's Hummingbird	
	Trogons (Trogonidae)	Elegant Trogon	
		Eared Quetzal	
	Hoopoes (Upupidae)	Eurasian Hoopoe	
	Kingfishers (Alcedinidae)	Ringed Kingfisher	
		Belted Kingfisher	
		Amazon Kingfisher	
		Green Kingfisher	
	Woodpeckers and Allies (Picidae)	Eurasian Wryneck	
		Lewis's Woodpecker	
		Red-headed Woodpecker	
		Acorn Woodpecker	
		Gila Woodpecker	
		Golden-fronted Woodpecker	
		Red-bellied Woodpecker	
		Williamson's Sapsucker	
		Yellow-bellied Sapsucker	
		Red-naped Sapsucker	
		Red-breasted Sapsucker	

	Great Spotted Woodpecker	
	Ladder-backed Woodpecker	
	Nuttall's Woodpecker	
	Downy Woodpecker	
	Hairy Woodpecker	
	Arizona Woodpecker	
	Red-cockaded Woodpecker	
	White-headed Woodpecker	
	American Three-toed Woodpecker	
	Black-backed Woodpecker	
	Northern Flicker	
	Gilded Flicker	
	Pileated Woodpecker	
	Ivory-billed Woodpecker	
Caracaras and Falcons (Falconidae)	Collared Forest-Falcon	
	Crested Caracara	
	Eurasian Kestrel	
	American Kestrel	
	Red-footed Falcon	
	Merlin	
	Eurasian Hobby	
	Aplomado Falcon	
	Gyrfalcon	
	Peregrine Falcon	
	Prairie Falcon	
Lories, Lovebirds, and Australasian Parrots (Psittaculidae)	Budgerigar	
	Rosy-faced Lovebird	
Parakeets, Macaws, and Parrots (Psittacidae)	Monk Parakeet	
	Carolina Parakeet	
	Nanday Parakeet	
	Green Parakeet	

		Thick-billed Parrot	
		White-winged Parakeet	
		Red-crowned Parrot	
Tyrant Flycatchers (Tyrannidae)		Northern Beardless-Tyrannulet	
		Greenish Elaenia	
		White-crested Elaenia	
		Tufted Flycatcher	
		Olive-sided Flycatcher	
		Greater Pewee	
		Western Wood-Pewee	
		Eastern Wood-Pewee	
		Cuban Pewee	
		Yellow-bellied Flycatcher	
		Acadian Flycatcher	
		Alder Flycatcher	
		Willow Flycatcher	
		Least Flycatcher	
		Hammond's Flycatcher	
		Gray Flycatcher	
		Dusky Flycatcher	
		Pacific-slope Flycatcher	
		Cordilleran Flycatcher	
		Buff-breasted Flycatcher	
		Black Phoebe	
		Eastern Phoebe	
		Say's Phoebe	
		Vermilion Flycatcher	
		Dusky-capped Flycatcher	
		Ash-throated Flycatcher	
		Nutting's Flycatcher	
		Great Crested Flycatcher	
		Brown-crested Flycatcher	

		La Sagra's Flycatcher	
		Great Kiskadee	
		Social Flycatcher	
		Sulphur-bellied Flycatcher	
		Piratic Flycatcher	
		Variegated Flycatcher	
		Crowned Slaty Flycatcher	
		Tropical Kingbird	
		Couch's Kingbird	
		Cassin's Kingbird	
		Thick-billed Kingbird	
		Western Kingbird	
		Eastern Kingbird	
		Gray Kingbird	
		Loggerhead Kingbird	
		Scissor-tailed Flycatcher	
		Fork-tailed Flycatcher	
	Becards, Tityras, and Allies (Tityridae)	Masked Tityra	
		Gray-collared Becard	
		Rose-throated Becard	
	Shrikes (Laniidae)	Brown Shrike	
		Loggerhead Shrike	
		Northern Shrike	
	Vireos (Vireonidae)	White-eyed Vireo	
		Thick-billed Vireo	
		Bell's Vireo	
		Black-capped Vireo	
		Gray Vireo	
		Yellow-throated Vireo	
		Plumbeous Vireo	
		Cassin's Vireo	
		Blue-headed Vireo	

	Hutton's Vireo	
	Warbling Vireo	
	Philadelphia Vireo	
	Red-eyed Vireo	
	Yellow-green Vireo	
	Black-whiskered Vireo	
	Yucatan Vireo	
Jays and Crows (Corvidae)	Gray Jay	
	Brown Jay	
	Green Jay	
	Pinyon Jay	
	Steller's Jay	
	Blue Jay	
	Florida Scrub-Jay	
	Island Scrub-Jay	
	Western Scrub-Jay	
	Mexican Jay	
	Clark's Nutcracker	
	Black-billed Magpie	
	Yellow-billed Magpie	
	Eurasian Jackdaw	
	American Crow	
	Northwestern Crow	
	Tamaulipas Crow	
	Fish Crow	
	Chihuahuan Raven	
	Common Raven	
Larks (Alaudidae)	Sky Lark	
	Horned Lark	

Family	Species	
Swallows (Hirundinidae)	Purple Martin	
	Cuban Martin	
	Gray-breasted Martin	
	Southern Martin	
	Brown-chested Martin	
	Tree Swallow	
	Mangrove Swallow	
	Violet-green Swallow	
	Bahama Swallow	
	Northern Rough-winged Swallow	
	Bank Swallow	
	Cliff Swallow	
	Cave Swallow	
	Barn Swallow	
	Common House-Martin	
Chickadees and Titmice (Paridae)	Carolina Chickadee	
	Black-capped Chickadee	
	Mountain Chickadee	
	Mexican Chickadee	
	Chestnut-backed Chickadee	
	Boreal Chickadee	
	Gray-headed Chickadee	
	Bridled Titmouse	
	Oak Titmouse	
	Juniper Titmouse	
	Tufted Titmouse	
	Black-crested Titmouse	
Verdin (Remizidae)	Verdin	
Bushtits (Aegithalidae)	Bushtit	
Nuthatches (Sittidae)	Red-breasted Nuthatch	
	White-breasted Nuthatch	
	Brown-headed Nuthatch	

Creepers (Certhiidae)	Brown Creeper	
Wrens (Troglodytidae)	Rock Wren	
	Canyon Wren	
	House Wren	
	Pacific Wren	
	Winter Wren	
	Sedge Wren	
	Marsh Wren	
	Carolina Wren	
	Bewick's Wren	
	Cactus Wren	
	Sinaloa Wren	
Gnatcatchers and Gnatwrens (Polioptilidae)	Blue-gray Gnatcatcher	
	California Gnatcatcher	
	Black-tailed Gnatcatcher	
	Black-capped Gnatcatcher	
Dippers (Cinclidae)	American Dipper	
Bulbuls (Pycnonotidae)	Red-whiskered Bulbul	
Kinglets (Regulidae)	Golden-crowned Kinglet	
	Ruby-crowned Kinglet	
Leaf Warblers (Phylloscopidae)	Willow Warbler	
	Common Chiffchaff	
	Wood Warbler	
	Dusky Warbler	
	Pallas's Leaf Warbler	
	Yellow-browed Warbler	
	Arctic Warbler	
	Kamchatka Leaf Warbler	
Sylviid Warblers (Sylviidae)	Lesser Whitethroat	
	Wrentit	
Reed Warblers (Acrocephalidae)	Sedge Warbler	

Grassbirds (Locustellidae)	Middendorff's Grasshopper-Warbler	
	Lanceolated Warbler	
Old World Flycatchers (Muscicapidae)	Gray-streaked Flycatcher	
	Asian Brown Flycatcher	
	Spotted Flycatcher	
	Dark-sided Flycatcher	
	Rufous-tailed Robin	
	Siberian Rubythroat	
	Bluethroat	
	Siberian Blue Robin	
	Red-flanked Bluetail	
	Narcissus Flycatcher	
	Mugimaki Flycatcher	
	Taiga Flycatcher	
	Northern Wheatear	
	Common Redstart	
	Stonechat	
Thrushes (Turdidae)	Eastern Bluebird	
	Western Bluebird	
	Mountain Bluebird	
	Townsend's Solitaire	
	Brown-backed Solitaire	
	Orange-billed Nightingale-Thrush	
	Black-headed Nightingale-Thrush	
	Veery	
	Gray-cheeked Thrush	
	Bicknell's Thrush	
	Swainson's Thrush	
	Hermit Thrush	
	Wood Thrush	
	Eurasian Blackbird	

	Eyebrowed Thrush	
	Dusky Thrush	
	Fieldfare	
	Redwing	
	Song Thrush	
	Clay-colored Thrush	
	White-throated Thrush	
	Rufous-backed Robin	
	American Robin	
	Red-legged Thrush	
	Varied Thrush	
	Aztec Thrush	
Mockingbirds and Thrashers (Mimidae)	Blue Mockingbird	
	Gray Catbird	
	Curve-billed Thrasher	
	Brown Thrasher	
	Long-billed Thrasher	
	Bendire's Thrasher	
	California Thrasher	
	Le Conte's Thrasher	
	Crissal Thrasher	
	Sage Thrasher	
	Bahama Mockingbird	
	Northern Mockingbird	
Starlings (Sturnidae)	European Starling	
	Common Myna	
Accentors (Prunellidae)	Siberian Accentor	
Wagtails and Pipits (Motacillidae)	Eastern Yellow Wagtail	
	Citrine Wagtail	
	Gray Wagtail	
	White Wagtail	
	Tree Pipit	

		Olive-backed Pipit	
		Pechora Pipit	
		Red-throated Pipit	
		American Pipit	
		Sprague's Pipit	
Waxwings (Bombycillidae)		Bohemian Waxwing	
		Cedar Waxwing	
Silky-flycatchers (Ptiliogonatidae)		Gray Silky-flycatcher	
		Phainopepla	
Olive Warblers (Peucedramidae)		Olive Warbler	
Longspurs and Snow Buntings (Calcariidae)		Lapland Longspur	
		Chestnut-collared Longspur	
		Smith's Longspur	
		McCown's Longspur	
		Snow Bunting	
		McKay's Bunting	
Wood-Warblers (Parulidae)		Ovenbird	
		Worm-eating Warbler	
		Louisiana Waterthrush	
		Northern Waterthrush	
		Bachman's Warbler	
		Golden-winged Warbler	
		Blue-winged Warbler	
		Black-and-white Warbler	
		Prothonotary Warbler	
		Swainson's Warbler	
		Crescent-chested Warbler	
		Tennessee Warbler	
		Orange-crowned Warbler	
		Colima Warbler	
		Lucy's Warbler	
		Nashville Warbler	

	Eyebrowed Thrush	
	Dusky Thrush	
	Fieldfare	
	Redwing	
	Song Thrush	
	Clay-colored Thrush	
	White-throated Thrush	
	Rufous-backed Robin	
	American Robin	
	Red-legged Thrush	
	Varied Thrush	
	Aztec Thrush	
Mockingbirds and Thrashers (Mimidae)	Blue Mockingbird	
	Gray Catbird	
	Curve-billed Thrasher	
	Brown Thrasher	
	Long-billed Thrasher	
	Bendire's Thrasher	
	California Thrasher	
	Le Conte's Thrasher	
	Crissal Thrasher	
	Sage Thrasher	
	Bahama Mockingbird	
	Northern Mockingbird	
Starlings (Sturnidae)	European Starling	
	Common Myna	
Accentors (Prunellidae)	Siberian Accentor	
Wagtails and Pipits (Motacillidae)	Eastern Yellow Wagtail	
	Citrine Wagtail	
	Gray Wagtail	
	White Wagtail	
	Tree Pipit	

	Olive-backed Pipit	
	Pechora Pipit	
	Red-throated Pipit	
	American Pipit	
	Sprague's Pipit	
Waxwings (Bombycillidae)	Bohemian Waxwing	
	Cedar Waxwing	
Silky-flycatchers (Ptiliogonatidae)	Gray Silky-flycatcher	
	Phainopepla	
Olive Warblers (Peucedramidae)	Olive Warbler	
Longspurs and Snow Buntings (Calcariidae)	Lapland Longspur	
	Chestnut-collared Longspur	
	Smith's Longspur	
	McCown's Longspur	
	Snow Bunting	
	McKay's Bunting	
Wood-Warblers (Parulidae)	Ovenbird	
	Worm-eating Warbler	
	Louisiana Waterthrush	
	Northern Waterthrush	
	Bachman's Warbler	
	Golden-winged Warbler	
	Blue-winged Warbler	
	Black-and-white Warbler	
	Prothonotary Warbler	
	Swainson's Warbler	
	Crescent-chested Warbler	
	Tennessee Warbler	
	Orange-crowned Warbler	
	Colima Warbler	
	Lucy's Warbler	
	Nashville Warbler	

	Virginia's Warbler	
	Connecticut Warbler	
	Gray-crowned Yellowthroat	
	MacGillivray's Warbler	
	Mourning Warbler	
	Kentucky Warbler	
	Common Yellowthroat	
	Hooded Warbler	
	American Redstart	
	Kirtland's Warbler	
	Cape May Warbler	
	Cerulean Warbler	
	Northern Parula	
	Tropical Parula	
	Magnolia Warbler	
	Bay-breasted Warbler	
	Blackburnian Warbler	
	Yellow Warbler	
	Chestnut-sided Warbler	
	Blackpoll Warbler	
	Black-throated Blue Warbler	
	Palm Warbler	
	Pine Warbler	
	Yellow-rumped Warbler	
	Yellow-throated Warbler	
	Prairie Warbler	
	Grace's Warbler	
	Black-throated Gray Warbler	
	Townsend's Warbler	
	Hermit Warbler	
	Golden-cheeked Warbler	
	Black-throated Green Warbler	

	Fan-tailed Warbler	
	Rufous-capped Warbler	
	Golden-crowned Warbler	
	Canada Warbler	
	Wilson's Warbler	
	Red-faced Warbler	
	Painted Redstart	
	Slate-throated Redstart	
	Yellow-breasted Chat	
Spindalises (incertae sedis)	Western Spindalis	
Tanagers (Thraupidae)	Bananaquit	
	Yellow-faced Grassquit	
	Black-faced Grassquit	
	White-collared Seedeater	
Emberizids (Emberizidae)	Olive Sparrow	
	Green-tailed Towhee	
	Spotted Towhee	
	Eastern Towhee	
	Rufous-crowned Sparrow	
	Canyon Towhee	
	California Towhee	
	Abert's Towhee	
	Rufous-winged Sparrow	
	Botteri's Sparrow	
	Cassin's Sparrow	
	Bachman's Sparrow	
	American Tree Sparrow	
	Chipping Sparrow	
	Clay-colored Sparrow	
	Brewer's Sparrow	
	Field Sparrow	
	Worthen's Sparrow	

	Black-chinned Sparrow	
	Vesper Sparrow	
	Lark Sparrow	
	Five-striped Sparrow	
	Black-throated Sparrow	
	Sagebrush Sparrow	
	Bell's Sparrow	
	Lark Bunting	
	Savannah Sparrow	
	Grasshopper Sparrow	
	Baird's Sparrow	
	Henslow's Sparrow	
	Le Conte's Sparrow	
	Nelson's Sparrow	
	Saltmarsh Sparrow	
	Seaside Sparrow	
	Fox Sparrow	
	Song Sparrow	
	Lincoln's Sparrow	
	Swamp Sparrow	
	White-throated Sparrow	
	Harris's Sparrow	
	White-crowned Sparrow	
	Golden-crowned Sparrow	
	Dark-eyed Junco	
	Yellow-eyed Junco	
	Pine Bunting	
	Yellow-browed Bunting	
	Little Bunting	
	Rustic Bunting	
	Yellow-throated Bunting	
	Yellow-breasted Bunting	

	Gray Bunting	
	Pallas's Bunting	
	Reed Bunting	
Cardinals, Piranga Tanagers and Allies (Cardinalidae)	Hepatic Tanager	
	Summer Tanager	
	Scarlet Tanager	
	Western Tanager	
	Flame-colored Tanager	
	Crimson-collared Grosbeak	
	Northern Cardinal	
	Pyrrhuloxia	
	Yellow Grosbeak	
	Rose-breasted Grosbeak	
	Black-headed Grosbeak	
	Blue Bunting	
	Blue Grosbeak	
	Lazuli Bunting	
	Indigo Bunting	
	Varied Bunting	
	Painted Bunting	
	Dickcissel	
Blackbirds (Icteridae)	Bobolink	
	Red-winged Blackbird	
	Tricolored Blackbird	
	Tawny-shouldered Blackbird	
	Eastern Meadowlark	
	Western Meadowlark	
	Yellow-headed Blackbird	
	Rusty Blackbird	
	Brewer's Blackbird	
	Common Grackle	
	Boat-tailed Grackle	

	Great-tailed Grackle	
	Shiny Cowbird	
	Bronzed Cowbird	
	Brown-headed Cowbird	
	Black-vented Oriole	
	Orchard Oriole	
	Hooded Oriole	
	Streak-backed Oriole	
	Bullock's Oriole	
	Spot-breasted Oriole	
	Altamira Oriole	
	Audubon's Oriole	
	Baltimore Oriole	
	Scott's Oriole	
Fringilline and Cardueline Finches and Allies (Fringillidae)	Common Chaffinch	
	Brambling	
	Asian Rosy-Finch	
	Gray-crowned Rosy-Finch	
	Black Rosy-Finch	
	Brown-capped Rosy-Finch	
	Pine Grosbeak	
	Eurasian Bullfinch	
	Common Rosefinch	
	House Finch	
	Purple Finch	
	Cassin's Finch	
	Red Crossbill	
	White-winged Crossbill	
	Common Redpoll	
	Hoary Redpoll	
	Eurasian Siskin	
	Pine Siskin	

	Lesser Goldfinch	
	Lawrence's Goldfinch	
	American Goldfinch	
	Oriental Greenfinch	
	Evening Grosbeak	
	Hawfinch	
Old World Sparrows (Passeridae)	House Sparrow	
	Eurasian Tree Sparrow	
Waxbills (Estrildidae)	Scaly-breasted Munia	

If you enjoyed this journal, we have many more styles and types to choose from. Visit our website for a complete list of journals.

www.wanderingwalksofwonder.com

National Parks Journal

Bucket List Journal

Kid's Travel Journal

Lighthouse Exploration Journal

Made in the USA
San Bernardino, CA
09 April 2018